Make Music With
The White Stripes

Complete Lyrics / Guitar Chord Boxes / Chord Symbols
Fifteen classic songs with a foreword by Alex Ogg

Published 2004

© International Music Publications Ltd
Griffin House 161 Hammersmith Road London W6 8BS England

Foreword: Alex Ogg
Music arranged and engraved by: Artemis Music Ltd
Cover Photograph: © Lex Van Rossen / Redferns Music Picture Library
All other photography: © Mick Hutson / Bob King / Martin Philbey / Jim Sharpe / Lex Van Rossen / Redferns Music Picture Library

Foreword

"If it's too good or if it's too fun or it's too enjoyable, just forget it."
Jack on The White Stripes' musical approach

It's unusual for contemporary rock 'n' roll, as regimented and steeped in implacable traditions and certainties as any art form in the early part of the 21st century, to gestate something quite as unique and reaffirming as the White Stripes. By soul-mining the American folk memory, travelling its back alleys and byways from Robert Johnson through the Delta bluesmen to Bob Dylan, punk rock and beyond, the White Stripes have become custodians of a lost language, defenders of a culture in a physical decline as marked as that of their home city, Detroit. In so doing they have done much to restore the purity of emotional attachment to the essential oils of music, rhythm and melody, unadorned by contrivances of marketing or salesmanship.

Jack and Meg, sensible, almost earnest types, are reassuringly singular in their dedication to their craft. They recognise the usefulness of mythology and symbol, and of holding something back from their audience in terms of their private lives, while investing everything in their music. Their efforts to disentangle the personal from the professional may not have been universally successful, given the scandal-lust and celebrity obsessions of the music media (mind you, dating film stars doesn't help). But thus far they have ensured nothing has got in the way of a wonderful quartet of albums, reinvesting traditional musical forms with visceral, gut-led authenticity. The results are thoroughly products of the modern era, an era that they somehow don't sound like they belong to.

It's hard to think of any within their peer group with such a clear grasp of their own plotline or presence. Think of contemporaries such as the Strokes and the instant mental image is of self-consciously cool young men shuffling through Greenwich Village. And that's about it, a monochrome trailer for the main feature. Think of the White Stripes and everything is widescreen and primary colours - the brother-sister-husband-wife tryst, the alchemy of red, black and white uniforms, the vintage 60s equipment, Jack's Ward's Airline guitar, Meg's bargain basement kit, an engrossing clash of innocence and suss, sweetness and smarts. The black hair. The pale skin. The beautiful exposition of contrast. And the sheer otherness of watching a man and a woman, who share a complex emotional history, belt it out with an underlying tension which intensifies and is intensified by the power of the music they make.

Jack White was born John Gillis in July 1975, the youngest of ten children in a blue collar Catholic family growing up in Ferdinand Street in the tough Mexicantown district of Detroit, an environment later celebrated in songs such as **Hotel Yorba, Screwdriver** and **I Think I Smell A Rat**. Music was a constant: he claims his six elder brothers had their own band, Catalyst, though this assertion has never been verified. By the age of five he could play the drums, before he formed his own band with childhood friend Dominic Suchtya at the local Holy Redeemer school. They would record songs in the attic together, using borrowed equipment to cut versions of Bob Dylan staples like **Masters Of War**.

They had moved on to blues standards, college rock staples, Led Zeppelin, and more exotically straight edge punks Fugazi, by the time both Gillis and Suchtya had moved on to the local Cass Tech. Jack also took a job as an apprentice upholsterer, through which he was educated in the ways of Detroit legends the MC5 and blues revivalists The Gun Club by Brian Muldoon, several years older, who sat in on the duo's rehearsals. White and Muldoon semi-officially became Two Part Resin when Suchyta left for college, though White also doubled up as drummer of Goober And The Peas, who had previously released a couple of independent albums, for their final tour. Ever industrious and independent-minded, he started his own business, Third Man Upholstery, but although he had a natural talent for the work, any long term success was made unlikely given his idiosyncratic billing protocols – clients would often be given invoices 'artistically' filled out in crayon. He also delighted in burying 'hidden' messages, to be discovered by his fellow upholsterers a few years down the line.

Megan White was born in November 1974 but came from a much more affluent area of town, Grosse Point. She was a shy but attentive student, with ambitions to study as a chef, before working the bar at dives like the Memphis Smoke, where one of her colleagues was Cory of Electric Six. She had no

musical ambitions until she met Jack. When the couple married in 1996, Jack defying convention by taking her surname, she started playing drums in the Gillis family home, which they took over from Jack's retiring parents. They would announce themselves as brother and sister – an illusion that would endure, with their own contrivance, for some time. It was never a 'band' as such. They just played along for laughs. Meg's technique was unfussy, untutored and direct, and that gave Jack a sense of purpose – he has talked widely of the benefits of operating 'within the box', of sticking to basics rather than dissipating the energy of the songs by compromising the touchstones of melody, rhythm and storytelling. As Jack confirmed to *Q* magazine, "Playing with another guy always leads into competitiveness. With Meg there was a different approach. She played drums in a whole new way. She wasn't trying to be loud or complex… and there was no clash of egos. What she did was just so simple, basic and uncluttered, which was so refreshing."

Their first show together was opening for the Hentchmen at local garage band haunt, the Gold Dollar. For the occasion they took the name White Stripes from a brand of peppermint candy. They were ragged, sure, but they created an instant impression. Surge Joebot of the Wildbunch later described the show as 'like something from Mars'. Also present at these early shows was Italy Records head and Young Soul Rebels' storeowner Dave Buick. After overcoming his bemusement at the group's line-up he was impressed, particularly by the duo's vivid stage apparel, best described as Elvis: The Satanic Years. He also picked up on the self-evident charisma of both participants. By the end of the year he'd invited them to cut a single for him. **Let's Shake Hands**, backed by the Marlene Dietrich cover **Look Me Over Closely**, was the result. Ben Blackwell, who helped out at Italy Records, reckons that while the a-side was fantastic, it wasn't a patch on the rest of their set. Pretty soon, Jack, the retired upholsterer, was part of a new set of furniture. He would help fellow travellers the Soledads as Italy's house producer, while also playing part time in other bands, Sub Pop artists The Go, whose debut album, **Whatcha Doin'?**, many consider the finest thing to emerge from Detroit in a generation, and rowdy country types Two Star Tabernacle, who cut a single with R&B veteran Andre Williams.

Their first dates outside Detroit followed after the single won over lo-fi darlings Pavement, who invited them on tour. They were initially intimidated by playing before crowds four or five times the norm, but grew to the challenge, even though they didn't make enough money to cover their expenses, despite Pavement helping out financially. **Lafayette Blues** followed, a tribute to the French origins of Detroit street names. Jack also hit on the arresting idea of including various denominations of French francs in initial copies, which also featured individual designs (copies have sold on e-bay for up to $1,000 subsequently). Though they remained small beer in Detroit, Italy Records was taking calls from all over the States. Much of their popularity was due to friends like Pavement, and other indie diehards like Sleater-Kinney, who took them on tour, as well as rockabilly punk veterans the Cramps and X. Later, Ryan Adams would claim the White Stripes made him want to "eat crack pipes and dance with the voodoo bones of the dead". They also reached the ears of Long Gone John, president of Californian punk label Sympathy For The Record Industry, via Steve Shaw of the Detroit Cobras. He put them in the studio to cut their first album with local engineer Jim Diamond, who had set up a ramshackle studio in a former poultry processing plant. The budget was just under $2,000. "I had Megan in one corner of the room where I set up an amp and a mic," Diamond later told Martin Roach, "because I wanted a big drum sound. For the vocals, Jack actually played through an old guitar amplifier, so it purposefully sounded dirty. Dirtier than it really was. Everyone does it now, they try to make it sound nastier than it really is. But this was a very direct way of recording."

"What's always been a question for us is: If we're breaking things down, how simple could they be? It seems to revolve around the number three - songwriting is storytelling, melody, and rhythm, those three components. If you break it down but you keep the three components, then you have what songwriting really is, without excess and overthinking."

Jack, to Jim Jarmusch, *Interview* Magazine

A rich cocktail of blues, rock and strained acoustic anguish, it featured three expressive covers in Dylan's **One More Cup Of Coffee** (from one of Jack's favourite albums, **Desire**), Robert Johnson's **Stop Breakin' Down** (made famous by the Rolling Stones, though Jack claimed he had never heard that version) and **St James Infirmary Blues**, recorded by Blind Willie McTell amongst many others. **Cannon** additionally featured a middle section based on Blind Willie Johnson's **John The Revelator**. Originals like the charming, childlike **Jimmy The Explorer** and the single, **The Big 3 Killed My Baby**, which pilloried Detroit's triumvirate of automotive empires, provided able original counterparts. In fact, three was "a big thing" for Jack, as he told Detroit's *Metro Times* in 1999. "It's three chords and three verses, and we accent threes together all through that. It was a number I always thought of as perfect, or our attempt at being perfect. Like on a traffic light, you couldn't just have a red and a green. I work on sculptures too, and I always use three colours." *Suzy Lee* was distinguished by the slide guitar of Johnny Walker, on temporary leave from the Soledads. The whole album was hallmarked, however, by its fearsome, minimal punch, Meg's spare, booming percussion providing the foundation for Jack's extraordinarily intuitive guitar playing. His singing, meanwhile, drew comparisons to Robert Plant's 'screaming woman' motif, especially on **Stop Breakin' Down**. He wasn't best pleased about that: Plant's singing was the thing he liked least about Led Zeppelin. This was a strange brew indeed from a city that was now synonymous with the eloquent brat-rap of Eminem and the techno movement, spearheaded by Juan Atkins *et al*.

The duo's second album took its title from Theo Van Doesburg's early 20th century Netherlands art movement, De Stijl. The sleevenote dedication was to Blind Willie McTell (whose **Your Southern Can Is Mine** was covered) as well as artist Gerrit Rietyeld (aka Rietvelt). The Rietyeld mention is instructive. He once described his most famous structure, the Schröder House (1924), thus: "I experimented with a construction frame where the units were not simply joined to each other, but continued in all three directions [three, as previously explained, is a big number in the White Stripes world]. My idea then was to close this space defining frame with two-dimensional surfaces. I experimented with three dimensional combinations of surfaces, combinations that were continuations, as it were, of the spatial frame: with as much contrast as possible between open and closed." A clear analogy for the White Stripes own music, as was Doesburg's exposition that he wanted to create a "spiritual reality" within De Stijl . His movement's insistence on clean, straight lines and primary colours similarly echoes through the White Stripes' work: the Schröder House has been called the world's 'least pretentious' building.

This time there was an expansion in styles, touching on straight pop and cabaret, with fleeting employment of violin and piano, though the way these were incorporated remained faithful to the White Stripes familiar 'purification through simplicity' dynamic. It was wholly recorded in Jack and Meg's house on Ferdinand Street, now renamed Third Man Studio. "To record at home was a bad idea," he later told *X-Ray*. "There were too many distractions – the phone ringing and all that jazz. And people knocking on the door. We even had some drunk guy walked in to the house off the street while we were recording **Death Letter**. He'd just wandered in because he heard us playing."

"Ringo knew what was needed, and he did what was right for the band, down to every little tiny thing needed for that song. And as much as I love all of the great drummers, there is that thing where it's about what the band needs. You know, when I hear music, I just hear the whole thing. I've never been much into picking things apart. It's the emotion of it that hits me, more than anything technical."

Meg, to Jim Jarmusch for *Interview* magazine

The highlights included the single, **You're Pretty Good Looking**, and the ferocious garage blur of **Hello Operator** (which was backed by a cover of Dolly Parton's **Jolene** when Sympathy For The Record Industry released it as a single). The latter featured harmonica from old Hentchmen sparring partner John Szymanski. Bruising in an altogether different sense was **Apple Blossom**, with its shockingly tender line "Put your troubles in a little pile and I will sort them out for you." If there had been any lingering doubt about Jack's abilities as a writer, this confirmed emphatically that he could turn his hand to more or less anything, he needn't hide behind the juggernaut that was his rhythm guitar playing. **Why Can't You Be Nicer To Me?**, with a nod to Captain Beefheart, was a nice, cynical counterpunch. Also in the front rank were the Son House cover **Death Letter** and two standout originals, **Sister, Do You Know My Name?**, with its melodic echoes of the Kinks, and the taut crowd-pleaser, **Let's Build A Home**.

The buzz surrounding the band was now tangible, but the White Stripes insisted on sticking to well understood and practised principles, of working within their 'box', structuring their response according to a pre-defined musical logic. But that did not mean stasis. So for **White Blood Cells** they took a step

back and consciously abandoned the blues-based formula that had established them, booking studio time in Memphis's Easley-McCain recording studios. "There's no blues on the new record," Jack told *Spin*. "We're taking a break from that. There's no slide work, bass, guitar solos, or cover songs. It's just me and Meg, guitar, drums and piano."

The results, recorded over just three days, lacked the immediacy of previous recordings, but were just as compelling. **Fell In Love With A Girl** skewered the kind of bubblegum garage pop that recalled Michigan's ? And The Mysterions' **99 Tears**. **Hotel Yorba** waxed nostalgic about a local Mexicantown establishment of decidedly ill repute, while drawing effectively on both country and folk traditions. Both **Same Boy You've Always Known** and **Offend In Every Way** were unequivocal statements of brute power. If **Dead Leaves And The Dirty Ground** was close to conventional hard rock in its surface aesthetics, **We're Going To Be Friends** had more in common with mid-period Beatles. **The Union Forever**, meanwhile, was a nod to Orson Welles and *Citizen Kane*, another long-term White obsession. Arguably the highlight, though, was the rugged, recalcitrant **I'm Finding It Hard To Be A Gentleman**, where the title's proposed restraint disappeared as the duo's familiar smouldering guitar and drum interplay took centre stage – rather like an argument between warring parents on a family day out. This was sophisticated, but still gut-wrenching stuff. Where the White Stripes had once produced primitive blues, now they were perfecting primitive rock 'n' roll and pop, a subtle but vital distinction.

White Blood Cells, premiered with three triumphant shows back at Neil Yee's Gold Dollar venue, was a significant international success, and some of the press focus extended to the underground Detroit garage scene from whence they'd sprung, meaning bands like the Dirtbombs, Soledad Brothers, Detroit Cobras, Von Bondies, Paybacks etc all got a slice of the coverage. All those acts featured on the **Sympathetic Sounds Of Detroit** compilation, the idea being that each act would perform using the same drums and amplifiers, recorded by Jack in his attic. For their part, both Jack and Meg were quick to stress that they'd developed out of an organic local scene, and were keen to help their fellow travellers where they could. As a direct consequence the Von Bondies were signed to a major, in this case by the legendary Seymour Stein. Interest was piqued in the UK by the patronage of John Peel, for whom they would cut their first session in the summer.of 2001. It proved a meeting of kindred spirits: Peel was delighted with their company as well as their music and, over food, was able to discuss the finer points of Lonnie Donegan and Gene Vincent without being made to feel old and irrelevant.

In August, specifically against their wishes, the *NME* slapped them on their front cover. Jack and Meg were worried that such undue early attention might deflect them from their intended trajectory. The *NME*'s Steve Chick countered that it was the paper's job to "blow things out of proportion". Fawning reviews were met with suspicion, not through ingratitude but simply because they did not welcome the distraction. But their newsworthiness certainly swelled audiences. The White Stripes were now guaranteed draws at every British venue they were booked at. As so often happens, it took the approval of the British media to convince music fans closer to home of the value of what they had. They were now evidently close to the top of the critical pile, totemic figureheads for the horribly named 'alt-rock' fanbase, who were just about over the Kurt and Courtney show but had been left shrugging their shoulders at Radiohead's left field truculence.

"We've never aspired to this level of attention. Look at all the money they spent. This is ridiculous. I don't know why we're doing this."

Jack, on the MTV Awards

The White Stripes had outgrown their independent status, and consequently signed a two-album deal with V2 in the US at the end of 2001, whose Andy Gershon had been won over after hearing **Hello Operator** on a tape. They were signed to XL, home of the Prodigy, in the UK for a £1 million advance. Their divorce with Sympathy For The Record Industry was ostensibly civil, despite the occasional hushed allegation about non-payment of royalties. Relatively amicable, too, was the duo's own divorce, though this didn't seem to have any undue effect on their professional relationship. They'd actually broken up shortly before playing The Blowout Festival in 1999, the *decree nisi* coming through a year later. At the time Jack had reportedly toyed with the idea of recruiting a new drummer, but eventually decided that the chemistry between them was worth persevering with. The highly observant may have noticed that their wedding rings had been airbrushed out of the artwork for

De Stijl. Jack later embarked on a relationship with Marcie of touring partners Von Bondies, although that turned sour after an altercation led to Jason Stollsteimer taking White to court for assault. White eventually pleaded guilty.

V2 re-released **White Blood Cells** in February 2002 and it flew out of stores, aided by rotation plays of **Fell In Love With A Girl** on MTV – despite the group's avowedly anti-corporate stance and suspicion of the music video format. They were, however, thrilled to play alongside Jeff Beck at his Royal Albert Hall shows in the UK in September, which preceded an invitation to support the Rolling Stones. As if that wasn't enough, Jack accepted a role in Anthony Minghella's American Civil War saga *Cold Mountain*, where he met future girlfriend Renee Zellweger. It could hardly have worked out better – he was recommended for the part by bluesman T-Bone Burnett, and much of the filming was shot in Transylvania. If this was all a little Hollywood for a group not known for Courtney Love-like courting of the camera, they did have the good sense to turn down a large sum of money to perform in a Gap advert. They were usually more impressed when they could meet their musical heroes – in Jack's case the bluegrass veterans he would create the soundtrack for *Cold Mountain* with, and nothing could have delighted Meg more than she and Jack being invited to stay at the ranch of her heroine, country star Loretta Lynn. Lynn's daughter had informed her the duo had dedicated **White Blood Cells** to her, and it proved to be a perfect match. She approved of their version of **Rated X**. "They sang it just like I did," she commented. "It was just different that a man did it instead of a woman. I think that (Jack) did a good job."

They also played Glastonbury in 1992 – one of the spectacles in the festival's long tradition of epic performances. On stage, you could just see them sucking in the history. And blowing it back out, too. As long-term followers of the band know, every show is different from the next. Jack, the one-man riff pylon, possesses a unique ability to improvise and reconstruct, and takes every opportunity to do so. Old blues licks from the group's extensive library weave in and out of the band's own compositions, which were never meant to sound exactly the same when repeated, the dynamics and acoustics changing with the venue and situation. It makes the White Stripes just about the least predictable and most satisfying live act of their generation.

Preparations for their fourth album included the notion that they'd go for something more reflective and musically soothing. Hmm. They would allow themselves ten days, and the recording would take place during spring 2003. In the event, they chose Toe Rag in Hackney, East London. because of strong testimonials they'd received about its eight-track equipment, some of it redundant technology rescued from Abbey Road. Jack was clearly enthused about the studio. "If someone says 'what are the great recordings in music,'" he told Mark Coles of Radio 1, "they'll be going back to things like Buddy Holly, Little Richard, Elvis Presley and James Brown. And they were all done with this same equipment. It was never surpassed in my mind. They never improved on analogue equipment."

"I like to imagine that children come into the world all innocent and kind-hearted and then slowly realize how hard and tough the surrounding world is. I am saddened when I see bad and arrogant people who are "uptight" the whole time, when they were once completely different from that. The worst is that most people seem to think that there is no other way, that it is set in stone. That is as good as continuing that meaningless search for a lower ideal, like money and all that other material crap. But I believe that one can work to become better, to become kinder and more empathetic."

Jack, to *Sonic* magazine

Mixing was completed at the end of the year as the duo continued to tour **White Blood Cells**. There was an incredible effort made to prevent the record being bootlegged and downloaded – instead of CDs, journalists were given vinyl copies, which had the added benefit of embarrassing those who had forsaken their turntables. Even trusted friends were told to wait for the release date. "When **Elephant** came along," John Peel recalled, "I listened to it and I thought they have taken that necessary next step, when people might have thought, 'Well, they're played out, they've done as much as they can do.' It's an LP that hangs together as an LP, and there's not a bad moment on it. I got the album a couple of months early, so I played a few tracks on it, and some lawyers from New York with the record label let it be known that legal action would be taken if I continued to play tracks from the record. I used to get this sort of thing in the days of Led Zeppelin, Pink Floyd and all that kind of stuff, but I'd thought, really, we'd grown out of that. I wanted to play it not out of any

sense of scooping anybody, but because, 'Hey, this is a great record - listen to it.' Not to be able to play it really upset me."

"Do not trust people who call themselves musicians or record collectors who say that they don't like Bob Dylan or The Beatles. They do not love music if those words come out of their mouths. They love record sleeves and getting attention for their hobby, but they don't love music."

Jack to *Mojo*

The resulting **Elephant** could hardly have been better realised. If anything, the quality control had tightened rather than slipped. The effect of the press focus on the band over preceding months seemed to result in a more insular and darker atmosphere. The mood was sombre, intimidating and, to an extent, unwelcoming. It featured one of the all-time great album openers in **Seven Nation Army**, a brooding agenda-setter, fired by Jack's distrust of the gossip and small-mindedness he'd encountered, with the kind of instant kick of Blur's **Song 2**, albeit with more staying power. Musically, many were convinced that the duo had finally relented and employed a bass player – the truth was that Jack had simply elected to play his guitar through an octave pedal. Those who want to know what the White Stripes might sound like with a bass player should check out Red Kross mainman Steve McDonald's cheekily re-edited MP3 versions, which actually amused the band. **Black Math**, driven on a relentless urchin riff and accompanying vocal histrionics, recalled the early 80s hardcore minimalism of Minor Threat or the Minutemen. **There's No Home For You Here** benefited from the judicious deployment of harmonies, and even drew some critical comparisons to Queen's **Bohemian Rhapsody**. The relentless thrust of **The Hardest Button To Button** was eclipsed by the full-blown blues jam **Ball And Biscuit**. "I do not really know what happened", Jack told *Sonic* magazine. "We were about to record **Ball And Biscuit**, which was written in the studio. All was peaceful and calm when, suddenly, it was as if the devil got into me and I could not hear anything except guitars. Fat, dirty, ear-destroying guitar sounds. It was as if some higher power said to me that now, Jack White, is the time to start playing guitar solos."

Shading arrived via the likes of **I Just Don't Know What To Do With Myself**, a reverent take on the Bacharach and David standard. Better still was Meg's vocal on **In The Cold, Cold Night**, a mood-altering downshift that had a similar effect to the Pogues' **I'm A Man You Don't Meet Everyday** on **Rum, Sodomy And The Lash**. "I wrote that specifically for Meg," Jack explained. "I wanted it to be half Mazzy Star and half Peggy Lee. I played it for her in my attic. Meg laughed, she liked it. That organ sound was from me lying down on the studio floor pressing the organ pedals. If you listen close you hear wood popping on the piano pedal."

"We take the stars from the blue union from heaven, the red from our mother country, separating it by white stripes, thus showing we have separated from her, and the white stripes shall go down to posterity representing liberty."

George Washington, later quoted in the insert to the White Stripes' debut single

If anyone thought they had forgotten their Detroit roots, **Little Acorns** featured a clip from local newscaster Mort Crim's *Second Thoughts* show. The lightest note was struck by **It's True That We Love One Another**, closing the album with the help of vocals from UK singer Holly Golightly and Meg – the title a playful jest at the music press which almost begged them to pursue more conjecture about the group's internal romantic dynamics.

If there was a theme it was a familiar one, as alluded to in the album's subtitle – Death Of The Sweetheart. In other words, Jack was fretting about the decline of intellectual rigour, manners, gallantry and defined roles in contemporary life. "It wasn't a political statement so much as a social idea about the attitude, you know - teenage girls with tattoos and body piercings, and the white boy from the suburbs who adopts a ghetto accent," he elaborated. "There's this whole attitude that you have to be hard, like, right out of the gate. And the sweetness and gentlemanly ideas are really going away. I'm sort of scared to bring up this notion, because I don't want it to sound like I'm some sort of conservative, old-fashioned person. But I've gotten the feeling that parenting and the way people are brought up now is getting away from these natural ideas and natural instincts in the male or female

personalities. They're being sacrificed for the idea of equality or good parenting, or relaxed parenting." Most of all he seemed to be mourning the loss of romance in the world, which provided further evidence of the conservative spine to a band perceived to be at music's cutting edge. Regardless, by the end of 2003, **Elephant** had sold more than three million copies worldwide.

They continued to tour, their ascent only interrupted in July when the news broke that Jack and Zellwegger had been involved in a car crash, Jack suffering a compound fracture of his left index finger. This naturally resulted in a long list of cancelled dates, but the problem was eventually rectified through surgery. Jack felt compelled to post pictures of the surgery on the band's website to prove that this wasn't some media stunt. He used the time productively, producing for Loretta Lynn. His mood was lifted, presumably, by the Grammys the White Stripes received for *Best Alternative Album* (**Elephant**) and *Best Rock Song* (**Seven Nation Army**). He might just as well have hated the recognition, though.

Meanwhile, the White Stripes had earned the approval of their greatest influence. Their appreciation of Bob Dylan had been signalled from the outset. The first recordings Jack made as a youth were covers of his work, and **One More Cup Of Coffee** made it on to the White Stripes' debut album. 17 March 2004 proved to be a very special occasion, as they were invited to support the great man on the last of his three shows in Detroit. Dylan even joined Jack on stage to run through **Ball And Biscuit**. It doesn't get any better than that for a music fan.

So, ladies and gentlemen, the White Stripes. They make music like it used to be made. More importantly, they make music like it ought to be made.

Alex Ogg lives in London with his partner Dawn and children Hughie and Laurence. Dawn proof-read this foreword but noted that, while it was generally OK, I'd missed out on Jack's big movie role in *School Of Rock*... Alex's books include **The Hip Hop Years**, **Top Ten** (both accompanying Channel 4 TV series of the same name), **Radiohead: Standing At The Edge**, **The Men Behind Def Jam**, **The History Of Rap Lyrics**, etc. He has also contributed to just about every music encyclopaedia ever published, including a couple that never made it to print, as well as the usual array of magazines and newspapers.

Discography:Albums

The White Stripes

Jimmy The Explorer
Stop Breakin' Down
The Big 3 Killed My Baby (CD)
Suzy Lee
Sugar Never Tasted So Good
(CD)
Wasting My Time
Cannon
Astro
Broken Bricks
When I Hear My Name
Do
Screwdriver
One More Cup Of Coffee (CD)
Little People
Slicker Drips
St James Infirmary Blues
I Fought Piranhas

Sympathy For The Record Industry
1999

De Stijl

You're Pretty Good Looking
(For A Girl)
Hello Operator
Little Bird
Apple Blossom
I'm Bound To Pack It Up
Death Letter
Sister, Do You Know My Name?
Truth Doesn't Make A Noise
A Boy's Best Friend
Let's Build A Home
Jumble, Jumble
Why Can't You Be Nicer To me?
Your Southern Can Is Mine

Sympathy For The Record Industry
2000

White Blood Cells

Dead Leaves And The Dirty
Ground
Hotel Yorba
I'm Finding It Hard To Be
A Gentleman
Fell In Love With A Girl
Expecting
Little Room
The Union Forever
The Same Boy You've Always
Known
We're Going To Be Friends
Offend In Every Way
I Think I Smell A Rat
Aluminium
I Can't Wait
Now Mary
I Can Learn
This Protector

XL
2001

Elephant

Seven Nation Army
Black Math
There's No Home For You Here
I Just Don't Know What To Do
With Myself
It's A Cold, Cold Night
I Want To Be With The Boy
You've Got Her In Your Pocket
Ball And Biscuit
The Hardest Button To Button
Little Acorns
Hypnotize
The Air Near My Fingers
Girl, You Have No Faith In
Medicine
It's True That We Love
One Another

XL
2003

Discography:Singles

Let's Shake Hands
b/w *Look Me Over Closely*
Italy
1997

Lafayette Blues
b/w *Sugar Never Tasted*
So Good
Italy
1998

The Big 3 Killed My Baby
b/w *Red Bowling Ball Ruth*
Sympathy For The Record Industry
2000

Hello Operator
b/w *Jolene*
Sympathy For The Record Industry
2000

Lord Send Me An Angel
b/w *You're Pretty Good Looking*
(Trendy American Remix)
Sympathy For The Record Industry
2000

Party Of Special Things To Do
b/w *China Pig*
Ashtray Heart
SubPop
2000

Hotel Yorba
b/w *X-Rated*
XL
2001

Fell In Love With A Girl
b/w *Let's Shake Hands*
Lafayette Blues
XL
2002

Dead Leaves And
The Dirty Ground
b/w *Suzy Lee*
Stop Breaking Down
XL
2002

Seven Nation Army
b/w *Good To Me*
Black Jack Davey
XL
2003

I Just Don't Know What To
Do With Myself
b/w *Lafayette Blues*
Black Math
XL
2003

The Big 3 Killed My Baby

Words and Music by
Jack White

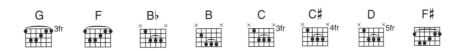

♩ = 77

Chorus   4/4 | G   F

The big three killed my baby,

| G   F

No money in my hand again.

| G   F

The big three killed my baby,

| G   F

Nobody's coming home again.

Verse 1 | G N.C.

Their ideas made me want to spit,

| F N.C.

A hundred dollars goes down the pit.

| G N.C.

30,000 wheels are rolling

| F N.C.

And my stick shift hands are swollen.

| G N.C.

Everything involved is shady.

| F N.C. | G

The big three killed my baby,

F | G   F

Yeah, yeah, yeah.

Chorus 2 | G   F

The big three killed my baby,

| G   F

No money in my hand again.

| G   F

The big three killed my baby,

| G   F

Nobody's coming home again.

Verse 2 | G N.C.

Why don't you take the day off and try to repair?

| F N.C.

A billion others don't seem to care.

| G N.C.

Better ideas are stuck in the mud.

| F N.C.

The motors running on truckers' blood.

| G N.C.

Don't let them tell you the future's electric

| B♭ N.C.

'Cause gasoline's not measured in metric.

| B N.C.

30,000 wheels are spinning

| C N.C.

And oil company faces are grinning.

| C♯ N.C.

Now my hands are turning red

| D N.C. | G

And I found out my baby is dead.

F | G   F

Yeah, yeah, yeah.

Chorus 3 | G   F

The big three killed my baby,

| G   F

No money in my hand again.

| G   F

The big three killed my baby,

| G   F

Nobody's coming home again.

Verse 3 | G N.C.

Well, I've said it now, nothing's changed:

| F N.C.

People are burning for pocket change,

| G N.C.

And creative minds are lazy,

| F N.C. | G

And the big three killed my baby,

F | G   F

Yeah, yeah, yeah.

Coda |G   F

        And my baby's my common sense

|G   F

        So don't feed me planned obsolescence.

|G   F

        Yeah, my baby's my common sense

|G   F

        So don't feed me planned obsolescence.

|G N.C. |F   F♯

        I'm about to have another blow-out.   /   /   /

|G N.C. |F   F♯ |G   ‖

        I'm about to have another blow-out.   /   /   /

Black Math

Words and Music by
Jack White

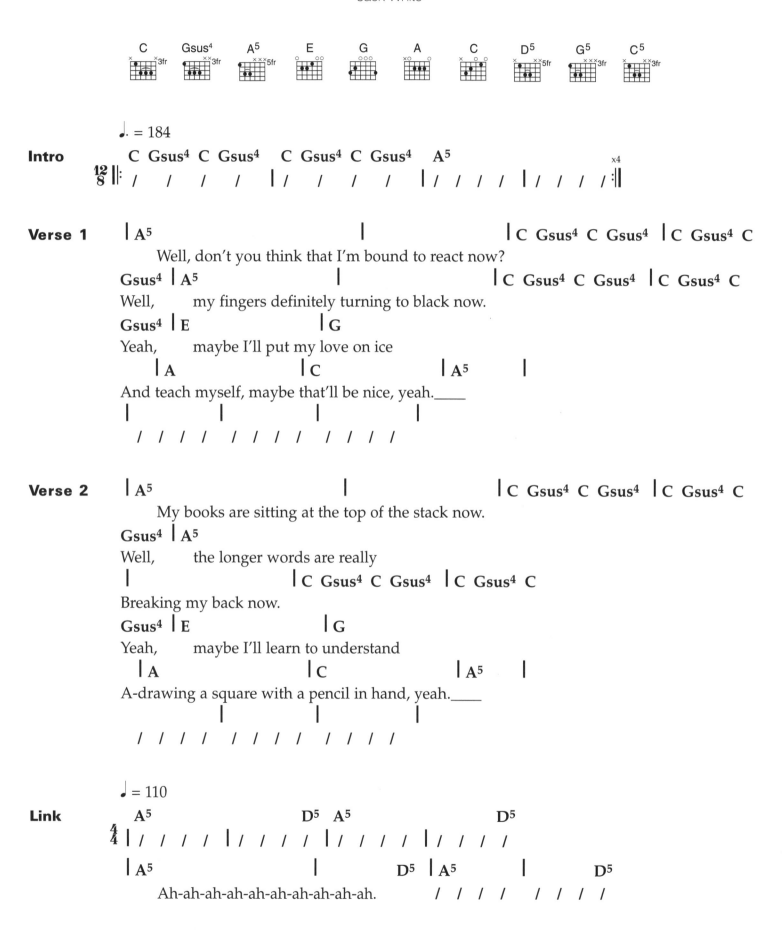

Bridge | A⁵ | D⁵

Mathematically turning the page,

| A⁵ | D⁵

Unequivocally showing my age,

| A⁵ | D⁵

I'm practically center-stage

| A⁵   D⁵

Undeniably earning your wage.

| E   G⁵

Well, maybe I'll put my love on ice,

| A⁵ | C⁵

Teach myself, maybe that'll be nice, yeah.

$\flat \cdot$ = 184

Link/solo   C Gsus⁴ C Gsus⁴   C Gsus⁴ C Gsus⁴   A⁵   x4

$\frac{12}{8}$ ‖: / / / / | / / / / | / / / / | / / / / :‖

A⁵

| / / / / | / / / / | / / / / | / / / / |

C Gsus⁴ C Gsus⁴   C Gsus⁴ C Gsus⁴   A⁵

‖: / / / / | / / / / | / / / / | / / / / :‖

A⁵

| / / / / | / / / / |

Verse 3 | A⁵ | | C Gsus⁴ C Gsus⁴ | C Gsus⁴ C

Listen master, can you answer a question?

Gsus⁴ | A⁵

Is it the   fingers or the brain

| | C Gsus⁴ C Gsus⁴ | C Gsus⁴ C

That you're teaching a lesson?

Gsus⁴ | E | G

Oh,   I can't tell you how proud I am:

| A | C

I'm writing down things that I don't understand.

| E | G

Well, maybe I'll put my love on ice

| A | C | A⁵ |

And teach myself, and maybe that'll be nice, yeah. / / / /

| N.C. | A⁵

/ / / Yeah.   / / / /

| N.C. | A⁵

/ / / Yeah.   / / / /

| N.C. | A⁵ | N.C. | A⁵ ‖

/ / / Yeah.   / / / / / / /

Dead Leaves And The Dirty Ground

Words and Music by
Jack White

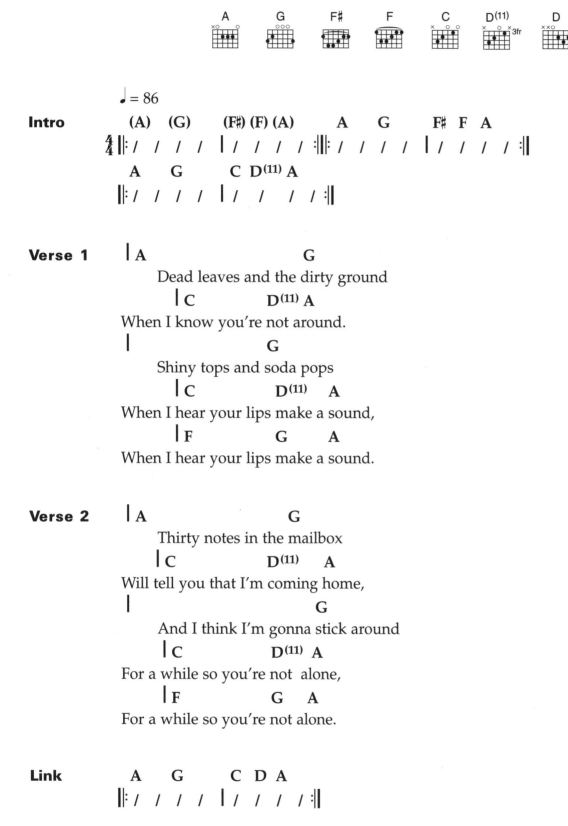

Verse 1

```
 A                        G
    Dead leaves and the dirty ground
    C          D(11) A
When I know you're not around.
                   G
    Shiny tops and soda pops
    C          D(11)   A
When I hear your lips make a sound,
    F         G    A
When I hear your lips make a sound.
```

Verse 2

```
 A                        G
    Thirty notes in the mailbox
    C          D(11)    A
Will tell you that I'm coming home,
                         G
    And I think I'm gonna stick around
    C          D(11)  A
For a while so you're not  alone,
    F         G    A
For a while so you're not alone.
```

Link

Verse 3 | A   (G)

        If you can hear a piano fall

           | (F♯)   (F)   A

You can hear me coming down the hall.

     | G

        If I could just hear your pretty voice

        | C   D(11)   A

I don't think I need to see at all,

        | F   G   A

Don't think I need to see at all.

Verse 4 | A   G

        Soft hair and a velvet tongue –

        | C   D(11)   A

I want to give you what you give to me.

     | G

        And every breath that is in your lungs

       | C   D(11) A

Is a tiny little gift to me,

       | F   G   A

Is a tiny little gift to me.

Link   A   G   C D A   D

||: /   /   /   / | /   /   /   / :|| /   /   /   /

Bridge | | A |

        I didn't feel so bad till the sun went down,   /   /   /   /

    | D |

        Then I come home –

                  | F

No-one to wrap my arms around,

        | G

Wrap my arms around.

Verse 3 | A   (G)

      Well, any man with a microphone
     | (F♯)   (F)   (A)
Can tell you what he loves the most.
     | G
      And you know why you love at all
      | C   D(11) A
If you're thinking of the Holy Ghost,
      | F   G   A
If you're thinking of the Holy Ghost.

Coda   A   G   C D A   A   G   C D A

Fell In Love With A Girl

Words and Music by
Jack White

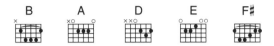

♩ = 95

Intro | B   A   D   E

4/4 | / / / / | / / / / |

Verse 1 | B   A

Fell in love with a girl:

| D   E

I fell in love once and almost completely.

| B   A

She's in love with the world

              | D | E

But sometimes these feelings can be so misleading.

| F♯   A

She turns and says, 'Are you alright?'

          | D   E

I said, 'I must be fine 'cause my heart's still beating.'

| F♯   A

'Come and kiss me by the riverside, yeah,

| F♯   N.C.

Bobby says it's fine – he don't consider it cheating, now.'

Verse 2 | B   A

Red hair with a curl,

        | D   E

Mellow roll for the flavour, and the eyes for peeping.

| B   A

Can't keep away from the girl.

        | D   E

I see stars in my brain, need a hallowed meeting.

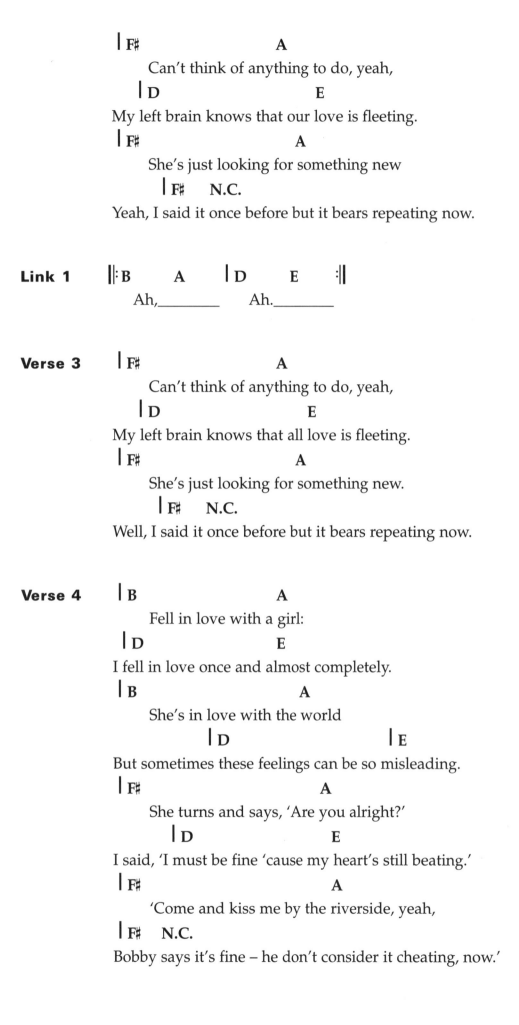

|F♯   A

   Can't think of anything to do, yeah,

 |D   E

My left brain knows that our love is fleeting.

|F♯   A

   She's just looking for something new

    |F♯ N.C.

Yeah, I said it once before but it bears repeating now.

Link 1 ‖:B A |D E :‖
       Ah,_____   Ah._____

Verse 3 |F♯   A

     Can't think of anything to do, yeah,

  |D   E

My left brain knows that all love is fleeting.

 |F♯   A

   She's just looking for something new.

   |F♯ N.C.

Well, I said it once before but it bears repeating now.

Verse 4 |B   A

     Fell in love with a girl:

 |D   E

I fell in love once and almost completely.

 |B   A

   She's in love with the world

    |D |E

But sometimes these feelings can be so misleading.

 |F♯   A

   She turns and says, 'Are you alright?'

   |D   E

I said, 'I must be fine 'cause my heart's still beating.'

 |F♯   A

   'Come and kiss me by the riverside, yeah,

 |F♯ N.C.

Bobby says it's fine – he don't consider it cheating, now.'

Link 2 ‖: B A | D E :‖
Ah,_____ Ah._____

Verse 5 | F♯ A

Can't think of anything to do, yeah,

| D E

My left brain knows that all love is fleeting.

| F♯ A

She's just looking for something new.

| F♯ N.C. | B ‖

Well, I said it once before but it bears repeating now.

The Hardest Button To Button

Words and Music by
Jack White

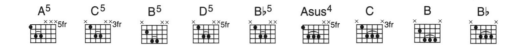

A⁵   C⁵   B⁵   D⁵   B♭⁵   Asus⁴   C   B   B♭

♩ = 128

Intro   (A⁵)

$\frac{4}{4}$ | / / / / | / / / / | / / / / | / / / / |

A⁵   C⁵   A⁵   C⁵

‖: / / / / | / / / / | / / / / | / / / / |

A⁵   C⁵   B⁵   D⁵

| / / / / | / / / / | / / / / | / / / / :‖

Verse 1 | A⁵ | C⁵

　　We started living in an old house

| A⁵ | C⁵

　　My Ma gave birth and we were checking it out.

　　| A⁵ | C⁵

It was a baby boy so we bought him a toy,

　　| B⁵ | D⁵

It was a ray gun and it was 1981.

　　　　| A⁵ | C⁵

We named him 'baby', he had a toothache:

　　| A⁵ | C⁵

He started crying, it sounded like an earthquake.

　　| A⁵ | C⁵

It didn't last long because I stopped it.

　　| B⁵ | D⁵

I grabbed a rag doll and stuck some little pins in it.

Prechorus　　　　　　　|A5　　　　　　　|C5

Now we're a family and we're alright now,
　　　　　|A5　　　　　　　　　|C5

We got money and a little place to fight now.
　　　　　　|A5　　　　　　　　　|C5

We don't know you and we don't owe you.
　　　　　　|B5

But if you see us around
　　　　　|B♭5

I got something else to show you.

Link　　　Asus4　N.C.　C　　　　N.C.　Asus4　N.C.　C　　　　N.C.

| / / /　| / / /　| / / /　| / / /　　|

　　Asus4　N.C.　C　　　N.C.　B　　　N.C.　B♭　　　N.C.

| / / /　| / / /　| / / /　| / / /　　|

(A5)

| / / / /　| / / / /　| / / / /　| / / / /　|

　A5　　　　　　C5　　　　　A5　　　　　　C5

| / / / /　| / / / /　| / / / /　| / / / /　|

　A5　　　　　　C5　　　　　B5　　　　　　D5

| / / / /　| / / / /　| / / / /　| / / / /　|

Verse 2　　　　　|A5　　　　　　　|C5

Now it's easy when you don't know better.
　　　　　　|A5　　　　　　　|C5

You think it's sleazy? Then put it in a short letter.
　　　　　　|A5　　　　　　　　|C5

We keep warm but there's just something wrong when you
　　　|B5　　　　　　　　　|B♭5

Just feel like you're the hardest little button to button.
　　　　　|A5　　　　|C5

I had opinions that didn't matter,
　　　　　　|A5　　　　|C5

I had a brain that felt like pancake batter.
　　　　　|A5　　　　　　|C5

I got a backyard with nothing in it
　　　　　|B5　　　　|B♭5

Except a stick, a dog and a box with something in it.

Chorus ‖:Asus⁴ N.C. | C N.C. :‖ ×4

The hardest button to button.

Chorus 2 ‖:Asus⁴ N.C. | C N.C. :‖ ×3

The hardest button to button.

B N.C. B♭ N.C. Asus⁴ (A⁵)

| / / / | / / / | / / / / |

Link 2 Asus⁴ (A⁵) C (C⁵)

| / / / / | / / / / | / / / / | / / / / |

Asus⁴ (A⁵) C (C⁵) D⁵

| / / / / | / / / / | / / / / | / / / / |

Chorus 3 ‖:Asus⁴ N.C. | C N.C. :‖ ×4 Asus⁴ ‖

The hardest button to button. / / /

Hotel Yorba

Words and Music by
Jack White

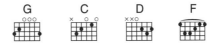

♩ = 97

Intro

G

4/4 | / / / / | / / /

Verse 1

| G

I was watching

| C

With one eye on the other side,

| D

I had 15 people telling me to move,

| G

I got moving on my mind.

|

I found shelter

| C

In some thoughts turning wheels around.

| D

I said thirty-nine times that I love you

| G

To the beauty I have found.

Chorus

| G

Well, it's one, two, three, four, take the elevator

| C

At the Hotel Yorba I'll be glad to see ya later

| D | G F G |

    All they got inside is vacancy.   /   /   /

Link 1

G   C   D   G

| / / / / | / / / / | / / / / | / / /

Verse 2 | G
I've been thinking
                      | C
Of a little place down by the lake:
                      | D
They got a dirty, old road

Leading up to the house
                      | G
I wonder how long it will take
                      |
'Til we're alone?
                      | C
Sitting on the front porch of that home,
| D
Stomping our feet on the wooden boards;
| G
We never got to worry about locking the door.

Chorus 2 | G
Well, it's one, two, three, four, take the elevator
                      | C
At the Hotel Yorba I'll be glad to see ya later
| D | G F G |
        All they got inside is vacancy.   /   /   /

Link 2   G   C   D   G
                | / / / / | / / / / | / / / / | / / /

Verse 3 | G
It might sound silly
                      | C
For me to think childish thoughts like these
                      | D
But I'm so tired of acting tough
                      | G
And I'm gonna do what I please.

26

|

Let's get married

    |C

In a big cathedral by a priest,

    |D

'Cause if I'm the man that you love the most

    |G

You can say 'I do' at least.

Chorus 3 |G

Well, it's one, two, three, four, take the elevator

    |C

At the Hotel Yorba I'll be glad to see ya later

|D |G

    All they got inside is vacancy.

Chorus 4 |G

And it's four, five, six, seven, grab your umbrella,

|C

Grab a hold of me 'cause I'm your favourite fella,

|D |G   C   G   D   G ‖

    All they got inside is vacancy.

I Just Don't Know What To Do With Myself

Words by Hal David
Music by Burt Bacharach

G   C   Am   Fsus⁴   Em   A   B♭⁵   C⁵   F⁵

♩ = 94

Intro

G   C   G   N.C.   G   C
4/4 | / / / / | / | / / / / |

Verse 1

| G N.C. | G   C | G
I just don't know what to do with myself,
N.C. | G   C | G
I don't know what to do with myself.
| Am |
Planning   everything for two,
| Fsus⁴ |
Doing   everything with you,
2/4 | Em   4/4 | A
And now that we're through
| G   C | G
I just don't know what to do._____

Verse 2

N.C. | G   C | G
I just don't know what to do with myself,
N.C. | G   C | G
I don't know what to do with myself.
| Am |
Movies   only make me sad,
| Fsus⁴ |
Parties make me feel as bad
2/4 | Em   4/4 | A
'Cause I'm not with you.
| G   C | G
I just don't know what to do._____

Bridge

N.C. | G

Like a summer rose

| | F5

    Needs the sun and rain,___

| | B♭5

    I need your sweet love

| F5 | C5 | C5

    To beat love away.   /

Verse 3

N.C. | G   C | G

Well, I don't know what to do with myself,

N.C. | G   C | G

Just don't know what to do with myself.

| Am |

    Planning everything for two,

| Fsus4 |

    Doing everything with you,

$\frac{2}{4}$| Em $\frac{4}{4}$| A

And now that we're through

          | G   C | G

I just don't know what to do._____

Bridge 2

N.C. | G

Like a summer rose

| | F5

    Needs the sun and rain,___

| | B♭5

    I need your sweet love

| F5 | C5 | C5

    To beat love away.   /

Coda

N.C. | G   F5 | G

I just don't know what to do with myself.

        | F5 | G

Just don't know what to do with myself.

        | F5 | G

Just don't know what to do with myself.

        | F5 | G   ‖

I don't know what to do with myself.

I'm Bound To Pack It Up

Words and Music by
Jack White

[Chord diagrams: D, Dsus⁴, F/D, Fsus⁴/D, G/D, Gsus⁴/D, C, G, F, D*]

Tune down a semitone

♩ = 85

Intro

D   Dsus⁴ D Dsus⁴ D F/D Fsus⁴/D F/D Fsus⁴/D F/D

$\frac{4}{4}$ ‖: / / / / / / | / / / / / / |

G/D Gsus⁴/D G/D Gsus⁴/D G/D D   Dsus⁴ D

| / / / / / / | / / / / / :‖

Verse 1

| D

I've thought about it for awhile

| F/D

And I've thought about the many miles

| G/D | D   Dsus⁴ D

But I think it's time that I've gone away.

|

The feelings that you have for me

| F/D

Have gone away it's plain to see

| G/D | D

And it looks to me that you're pulling away.

Chorus

| C   G

I'm gonna pick   it up,

| C   G | D Dsus⁴ D | Dsus⁴ D

I'm gonna pick   it up today.____

| C   G

I'm bound to pack   it up,

| C   G | F | G

I'm bound to pack   it up and go away.   / / / /

Link D Dsus⁴ D Dsus⁴ D F/D Fsus⁴/D F/D Fsus⁴/D F/D

‖: / / / / / / | / / / / / |

G/D Gsus⁴/D G/D Gsus⁴/D G/D D Dsus⁴ D

| / / / / / / / | / / / / :‖

Verse 2 | D

I find it hard to say to you

| F/D

That this is what I have to do

| G/D | D Dsus⁴ D

But there is no way that I'm gonna stay.

|

There's so many things you need to know

| F/D

And I wanna tell you before I go

| G/D | D Dsus⁴ D

But it's hard to think of just what to say.

Chorus 2 | C G

I'm gonna pick it up,

| C G | D Dsus⁴ D | Dsus⁴ D

I'm gonna pick it up today.____

| C G

I'm bound to pack it up,

| C G | F | G

I'm bound to pack it up and go away. / / / /

Verse 3 | D

I'm sorry to leave you all alone;

| F/D

You're sitting silent by the phone

| G/D | D Dsus⁴ D

But we've always known there would come a day.

|

The bus is warm and softly lit,

| F/D

And a hundred people ride in it;

| G/D | D Dsus⁴ D Dsus⁴ D

I guess I'm just another running away. / /

Chorus 3 | C   G

I'm gonna pick   it up,

| C   G | D $Dsus^4$ D | $Dsus^4$ D

I'm gonna pick   it up today.

| C   G

I'm bound to pack   it up,

| C   G | F

I'm bound to pack   it up and go away.

| G | D $Dsus^4$ D $Dsus^4$ D

Oh yeah, yeah._____

Coda   F/D $Fsus^4$/D F/D $Fsus^4$/D F/D G/D $Gsus^4$/D G/D $Gsus^4$/D G/D   D*

| / / /   /   / | / / /   /   / | ‖

I'm Finding It Hard To Be A Gentleman

Words and Music by
Jack White

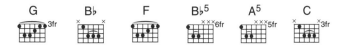

G   B♭   F   B♭5   A5   C

♩ = 80

Verse 1 $\frac{4}{4}$ N.C. |G

Well, I'm finding it harder

     B♭   F |G

To be a gentleman every day:

     |B♭   F

All the manners that I've been taught

       |G

Have slowly died away.

     |F

But if I held the door open for you

       |G

It would make your day, yeah.

Link   G   B♭ F   B♭5 A5 G   G

‖: / / / / | / /   / / :‖ / / / / |

Verse 2 |G |

       You think that I care

    B♭   F |G

About me and only me,

     |B♭

When every single girl

     F |G

Needs help climbing up a tree.

     |F |G

Well, I know it don't take much to satisfy me.

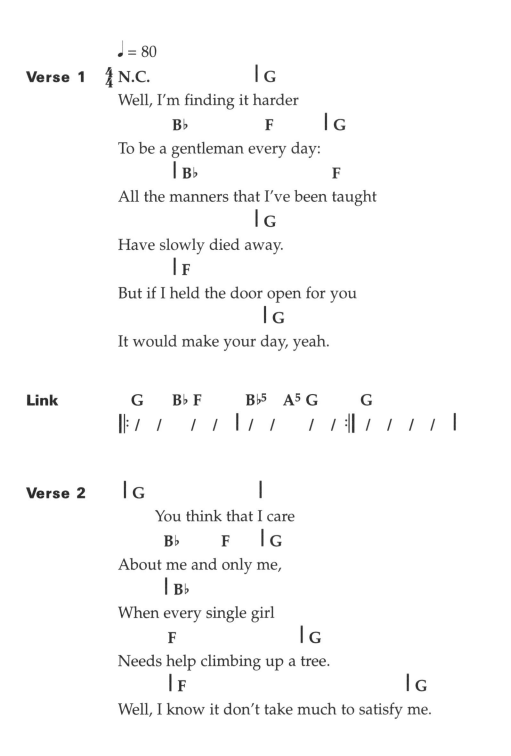

Link 2   G   B♭ F   B♭5 A5 G

‖: / /   / / | / /   / / :‖

Bridge | C | B♭
    Maybe it's whatever's in my hand
         | G
That's distracting me,
  | | B♭
    But if I could find emotion
  | C
To stimulate devotion,
        | D | D N.C.
Well, then you'd see.   / / /

Link 3   G   B♭ F   B♭5 A5 G   G

‖: / /   / / | / /   / / :‖ / / / / |

Verse 4 | G |
    Well, I'm finding it hard to say
    B♭   F | G
That I need you twenty times a day;
  | B♭
I feel comfortable,
    F | G
So baby why don't you feel the same?
    | F
Have a doctor come and visit us
| N.C. | G
    And tell us which one is sane.

Link 4   G   B♭ F   B♭5 A5 G   G

‖: / /   / / | / /   / / :‖ / / / / |

Verse 5 | G |

          Well, I never said I wouldn't

                B♭   F | G

Throw my jacket in the mud for you

          | B♭

But my father gave it to me,

      F | G

So maybe I should carry you.

             | F

Then you said, "You almost dropped me",

            | N.C.

So then I did

                   | G   ‖

And I got mud on my shoes.

Jumble, Jumble

Words and Music by
Jack White

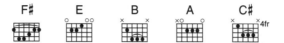

♩ = 164

Intro

```
          F#   E     F#   E          F#   E     F#   E  N.C.
 4 | / / / / | / / /  (Alright). | / / / / | / / /         |
 4

          F#   E     F#   E  N.C.    F#   E     F#   E
   | / / / / | / / /         | / / / / | / / /
```

Verse 1   N.C. | F#   E | F# E

Jumble, jumble

N.C. | F#   E | F# E

Out at my house,

N.C. | B   A | B   A

Come on over,

N.C. | F#   E | F# E

Sleep on the couch.

N.C. | C#

Can't even see ya –

| B | F#   E | F# E

Look like a mouse.

Link   F# N.C.   x4 F#   E   F#   E N.C. x3

```
|: / / / / | / / / / :|| / / / / | / / / :||
```

```
   F#   E     F#   E
 | / / / / | / / /
```

Verse 2   N.C. | F♯   E | F♯   E

Crumble, crumble:

N.C. | F♯   E | F♯   E

That bag is brown.

N.C. | B   A | B   A

Rip up the paper

N.C. | F♯   E | F♯   E

To hear a sound,

      | C♯

Pick the pieces

| B | F♯   E | F♯   E

    Up off the ground.

Link 2   F♯ N.C.   x4 F♯   E   F♯   E N.C.

‖: / / / / | / / / / :‖ / / / / | / / /

    F♯   E   F♯   E

| / / / / | / / /

Verse 3   N.C. | F♯   E | F♯   E

Tumble, tumble

N.C. | F♯   E | F♯   E

Onto the   floor,

N.C. | B   A | B   A

Roll   over

N.C. | F♯   E | F♯   E

Until you're poor.

      | C♯

Wave to me –

| B | F♯   E | F♯   E | F♯ ‖

    I'm at the door.

Seven Nation Army

Words and Music by
Jack White

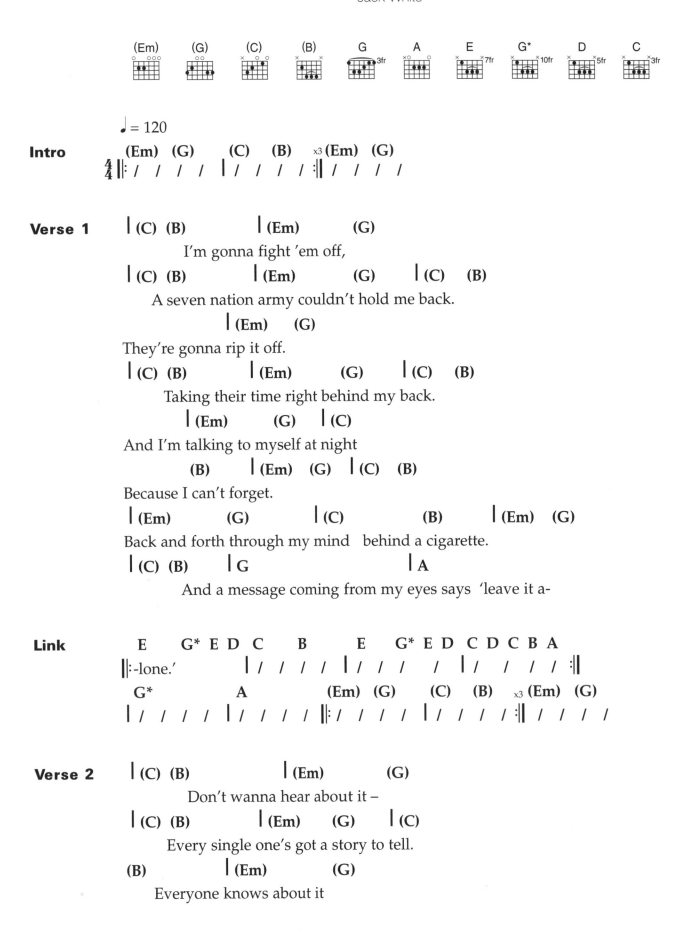

Intro

(Em) (G)   (C) (B)   x3 (Em) (G)

Verse 1

| (C) (B) | (Em)   (G)

I'm gonna fight 'em off,

| (C) (B) | (Em)   (G) | (C)   (B)

A seven nation army couldn't hold me back.

| (Em)   (G)

They're gonna rip it off.

| (C) (B) | (Em)   (G) | (C)   (B)

Taking their time right behind my back.

| (Em)   (G) | (C)

And I'm talking to myself at night

(B) | (Em) (G) | (C)   (B)

Because I can't forget.

| (Em)   (G) | (C)   (B) | (Em) (G)

Back and forth through my mind   behind a cigarette.

| (C) (B) | G | A

And a message coming from my eyes says 'leave it a-

Link

E   G* E D C   B   E   G* E D C D C B A

|: -lone.'

G*   A   (Em) (G)   (C) (B)   x3 (Em) (G)

Verse 2

| (C) (B) | (Em)   (G)

Don't wanna hear about it –

| (C) (B) | (Em)   (G) | (C)

Every single one's got a story to tell.

(B) | (Em)   (G)

Everyone knows about it

| (C) (B) | (Em)   (G) | (C)   (B)

From the Queen of England to the hounds of hell.

| (Em)   (G) | (C)

And if I catch you coming back my way,

(B) | (Em) (G) | (C)   (B)

I'm gonna serve it to you.

| (Em)   (G) | (C)

And that ain't what you want to hear

(B) | (Em)   (G)

But that's what I'll do.

| (C) (B) | G | A

And a feeling coming from my bones says 'find a

Guitar solo E   G* E D C   B   E   G* E D C D C B A ₓ4

‖: home.' | / / / / / | / / /   / | / /   / / / :‖

G*   A   (Em) (G)   (C)   (B)   ₓ3 (Em) (G)

| / / / / / | / / / / / ‖: / / / / | / / / / / :‖ / / / /

Verse 3 | (Em)   (G)

I'm going to Wichita

| (C) (B) | (Em)   (G) | (C)   (B)

Far from this opera forever more.

| (Em)   (G)

I'm gonna work the straw,

| (C) (B) | (Em)   (G) | (C)   (B)

Make the sweat drip out of every pore.

| (Em)   (G)

And I'm bleeding, and I'm bleeding,

| (C)   (B) | (Em)   (G)

And I'm bleeding right before my Lord.

| (C) (B) | (Em)   (G) | (C)

All the words are gonna bleed from me,

(B) | (Em)   (G)

And I will think no more.

| (C) (B) | G | A

And the stains coming from my blood tell me 'go back

Link/Coda   E   G* E D C   B   E   G* E D C D C B A   E

‖: home.' | / / / / / | / / /   / | / /   / / / :‖ /   ‖

Stop Breaking Down

Words and Music by
Jack White

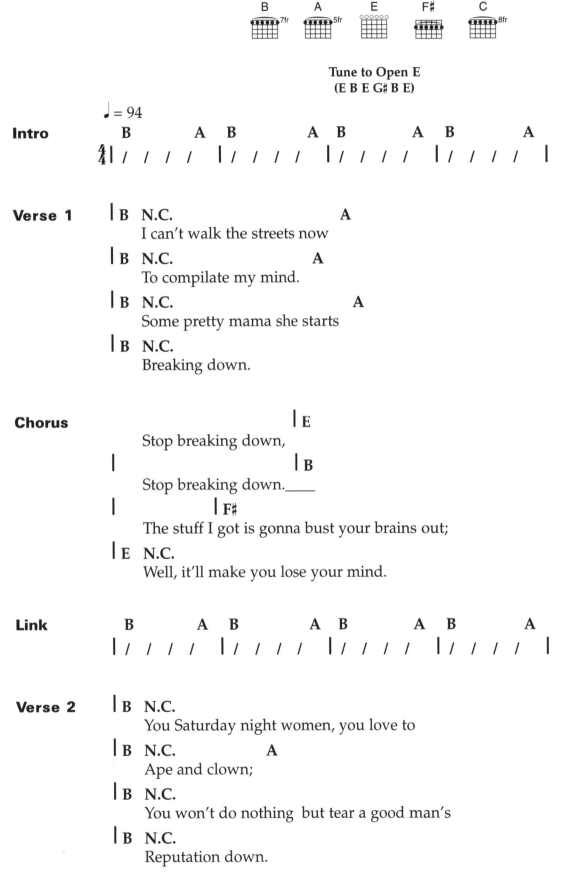

Tune to Open E
(E B E G♯ B E)

♩ = 94

Intro
B   A   B   A   B   A   B   A

4/4

Verse 1
│ B   N.C.   A
I can't walk the streets now

│ B   N.C.   A
To compilate my mind.

│ B   N.C.   A
Some pretty mama she starts

│ B   N.C.
Breaking down.

Chorus
                              │ E
Stop breaking down,

│   │ B
Stop breaking down.____

│   │ F♯
The stuff I got is gonna bust your brains out;

│ E   N.C.
Well, it'll make you lose your mind.

Link
B   A   B   A   B   A   B   A

Verse 2
│ B   N.C.
You Saturday night women, you love to

│ B   N.C.   A
Ape and clown;

│ B   N.C.
You won't do nothing but tear a good man's

│ B   N.C.
Reputation down.

Chorus 2

                   | E

Stop breaking down,

| | B

Stop breaking down.____

| | F#

The stuff I got is gonna bust your brains out;

| E N.C.

Well, it'll make you lose your mind.

Link 2   B   A B   A

| / / / / | / / / / |

Guitar solo B   A B   C B   A B A B A

| / / / / | / / / / | / / / | / / / / |

  E   B

| / / / / | / / / / | / / / / | / / / / |

  F#   A   B   A B   A

| / / / / | / / / / | / / / / | / / / / |

Verse 3 | B   A

I gave my baby

| B   A

The 99th degree,

| B

She jumped up and threw a pistol

|

Down on me.

Chorus 3

                   | E

Stop breaking down,

| | B

Yeah, stop breaking down.____

| | F#

The stuff I got is gonna bust your brains out;

| E N.C.   B ‖

Well, it'll make you lose your mind.

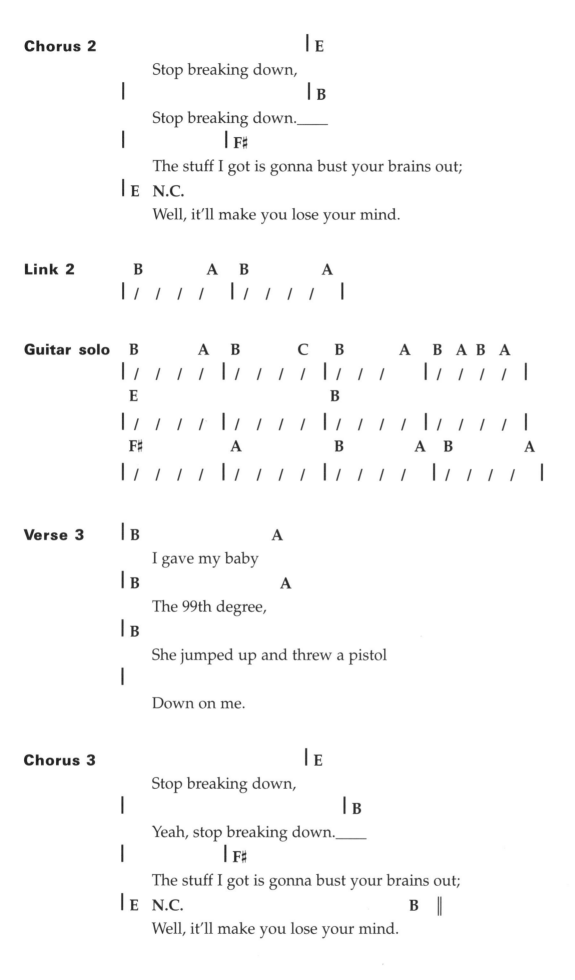

There's No Home For You Here

Words and Music by
Jack White

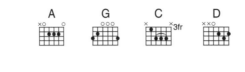

♩ = 75

Intro $\frac{4}{4}$ | A   G | C   A   G

Ah._____

Chorus | A   G

There's no home for you here girl, go away,

| C   A   G

There's no home for you here.

| A   G

There's no home for you here girl, go away,

| C   A   G

There's no home for you here.

Link 1   A   G   C   A G x3

Verse 1 | A   G

I'd like to think that all this constant interaction

| C   A   G

Is just the kind to make you drive yourself away.

| A   G

Each simple gesture done by me is counter-acted,

| C   A   G

Leaves me standing here with nothing else to say.

| A   G

Completely baffled by a backward indication

| C   A   G

That an inspired word will come across your tongue.

| A   G

Hands moving upward to propel the situation

| C   A   G

Have simply halted now the conversation's   done.

Chorus 2 | A   G

    There's no home for you here girl, go away,

    | C   A   G

    There's no home for you here.

    | A   G

    There's no home for you here girl, go away,

    | C   A   G

    There's no home for you here.

Link 2   A   G   C   A G

    ‖: / / / / | / / / / :‖

Verse 3 | A   G

    I'm only waiting for the proper time to tell you

        | C   A   G

That it's impossible to get along with you.

    | A   G

    It's hard to look you in the face when we are talking

     | C   A   G

So it helps to have a mirror in the room.

    | A   G

    I've not been really looking forward to the performance

        | C   A   G

But there's my cue and there's a question on your face.

    | A   G

    Fortunately I have come across an answer

     | C   A   G

Which is go away and do not leave a trace.

Link 3   N.C.

    Ah._____

Chorus 3   N.C.

There's no home for you here girl, go away,

There's no home for you here.

There's no home for you here girl, go away,

There's no home for you here.

Solo

```
        A    G       C      A  G  A    G       C       A
 ‖: /  /   /   /  | /  /   /   /  :‖ /  /   /   /  | /   /   /   /  |
```

Bridge | D

Waking up for breakfast, burning matches, talking quickly,
            |

Breaking baubles, throwing garbage, drinking soda,
                               | C   G

Looking happy, taking pictures, so completely stupid, just go away.
 | A   G

   Ah._____

Link 4

```
        A    G       C      A  G
 ‖: /  /   /   /  | /  /   /   /  :‖
```

Chorus 4 | A   G

   There's no home for you here girl, go away,
 | C   A   G

   There's no home for you here.
 | A   G

   There's no home for you here girl, go away,
 | C   A   G

   There's no home for you here.

   repeat ad lib. to fade

You've Got Her In Your Pocket

Words and Music by
Jack White

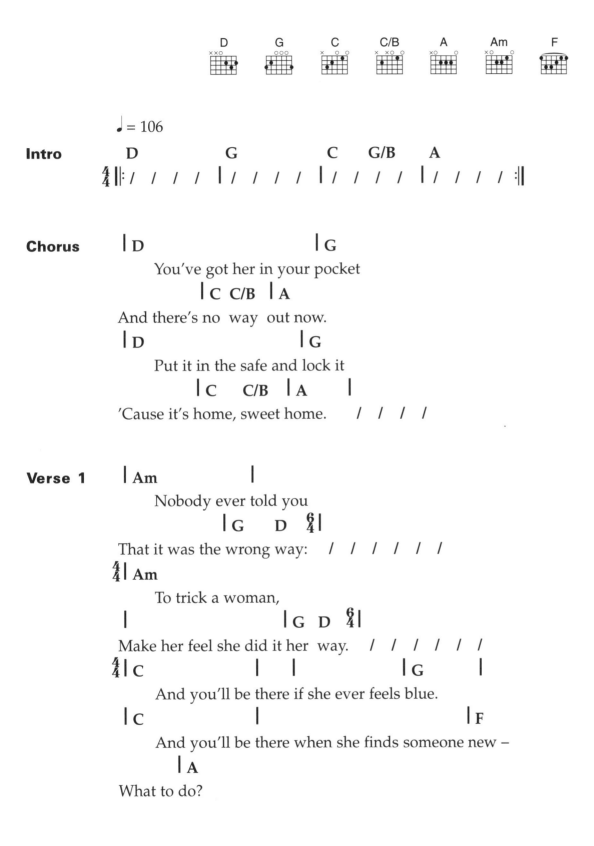

♩ = 106

Intro

D　　　　　G　　　　　C　G/B　A

4/4 ‖: / / / / | / / / / | / / / / | / / / / :‖

Chorus

| D　　　　　　　| G
You've got her in your pocket
　　　　　　| C　C/B　| A
And there's no　way　out now.
| D　　　　　　　| G
Put it in the safe and lock it
　　　　　　| C　　C/B　| A　　　　|
'Cause it's home, sweet home.　　　/　/　/　/

Verse 1

| Am　　　　　　　|
Nobody ever told you
　　　　　| G　　D　6/4|
That it was the wrong way:　/　/　/　/　/　/
4/4| Am
To trick a woman,
|　　　　　　　　　| G　D　6/4|
Make her feel she did it her　way.　/　/　/　/　/　/
4/4| C　　　　　|　　|　　　　　| G　　　|
And you'll be there if she ever feels blue.
| C　　　　　|　　　　　　　　|F
And you'll be there when she finds someone new –
　　　　| A
What to do?

Chorus 2 | D | G

Well you know you keep her in your pocket
                 | C   C/B | A

Where there's no   way out now.
| D | G

    Put it in the safe and lock it
            | C   C/B | A | | Am |

'Cause it's home, sweet home.   / / / / / / / / / / / /

Verse 2 | Am |

    The smile on your face
                 | G   D $\frac{6}{4}$|

Made her think she had the right one,   / / / / / /
$\frac{4}{4}$| Am |

    Then she thought she was sure
              | G   D $\frac{6}{4}$|

By the way you two could have fun.   / / / / / /
$\frac{4}{4}$| C |

    But now she might leave
             | G |

Like she's threatened before.   / / / /
| C | | F

    Grab hold of her fast before her feet leave the floor
             | A

And she's out the door.

Chorus 3 | D | G

'Cause you want to keep her in your pocket
                | C   C/B | A

Where there's no way out now.
| D | G

    Put it in the safe and lock it
            | C   C/B | A | | Am |

'Cause it's home, sweet home.   / / / / / / / / / / / /

Verse 3 | Am |

        And in your own mind you know

              | G   D $\frac{6}{4}$|

You're lucky just to know her,   / / / / / /

$\frac{4}{4}$| Am |

        And in the beginning

              | G   D $\frac{6}{4}$|

All you wanted was to show her.   / / / / / /

$\frac{4}{4}$| C |

        But now you're scared –

              | G |

You think she's running away;   / / / /

| C | | F

        You search in your hand for something clever to say.

        | A

Don't go away.

Chorus 4 | D | G

'Cause I want to keep you in my pocket

          | C C/B | A

Where there's no way out now.

| D | G

        Put it in the safe and lock it

          | C   C/B | A

'Cause it's home, sweet home.

| C   C/B | A   ‖

Home, sweet home.

You're Pretty Good Looking

Words and Music by
Jack White

B   E   F♯   A♯   C   C♯   D   D♯   G♯

♩ = 115

Intro

B   F♯

4/4 | / / / / | / / / / | / / / / |

Verse 1

| B N.C. | B | E
Oh yeah, you're pretty good looking for a girl
      F♯ | B
But your back is so broken,
| | | E
And this feeling's still gonna linger on
   F♯ | B   E | F♯
Until the year Twenty-five twenty-five now.

Verse 2

N.C. | B | E
Yeah, you're pretty good looking for a girl:
   F♯ | B
Your eyes are wide open,
| | | E
And your thoughts have been stolen by the boys
F♯ | B   E | F♯
Who took you out and bought you everything you want now.

Chorus

N.C. | B | E
Yeah, you're pretty good looking, oh yeah.
    F♯ | B
You're pretty good looking.
| | | E
Yes, you're pretty good looking, oh yeah,
F♯ | B F♯ | B A♯ B C C♯ D
For a girl.

Bridge
   | D♯ |
      Lots of people in this world
    | G♯ |
But I wanna be your boy.
   | C♯ |
      To me that thought is sounding so absurd
     | E   F♯
And I don't wanna be your toy.

Verse 3   N.C. | B | E
      'Cause you're pretty good looking for a girl.
      F♯ | B
My future's wide open
 | | | E
      But this feeling's still gonna linger on
    F♯ | B   E | F♯
Until I know everything I need to know now.

Chorus 2   N.C. | B | E
Yeah, you're pretty good looking, oh yeah.
      F♯ | B
You're pretty good looking.
 | | | E
      Yes, you're pretty good looking, oh yeah,
F♯ | B   F♯ | B   ‖
For a girl.

Songs guitars were meant to play

Essential Acoustic Playlist 2
9854A   VC   ISBN: 1-84328-411-1

A Minha Meninha (The Bees) – Ain't That Enough (Teenage Fanclub) – All Together Now (The Farm) – Alright (Supergrass) – Am I Wrong (Mull Historical Society) – American English (Idlewild) – Average Man (Turin Brakes) – Beetlebum (Blur) – Breakfast at Tiffany's (Deep Blue Something) – Buy It In Bottles (Richard Ashcroft) – Can You Dig It? (The Mock Turtles) – Caught By The River (Doves) – Coffee & TV (Blur) – Come Away With Me (Norah Jones) – Come Back To What You Know (Embrace) – Common People (Pulp) – Crazy Beat (Blur) – Creep (Radiohead) – A Design For Life (Manic Street Preachers) – Distant Sun (Crowded House) – Don't Let Me Down Gently (The Wonderstuff) – Don't Think You're The First (The Coral) – Everlong (Foo Fighters) – Fallen Angel (Elbow) – Fastboy (The Bluetones) – The Final Arrears (Mull Historical Society) – Forget About Tomorrow (Feeder) – Getting Away With It (Electronic) – Go To Sleep (Radiohead) – Grace (Supergrass) – Here's Where The Story Ends (The Sundays) – High And Dry (Radiohead) – History (The Verve) – Hooligan (Embrace) – I Need Direction (Teenage Fanclub) – I Will (Radiohead) – (I'm Gonna) Cry Myself Blind (Primal Scream) – In A Room (Dodgy) – It's True That We Love One Another (The White Stripes) – Just When You're Thinkin' Things Over (The Charlatans) – La Breeze (Simian) – Lilac Wine (Jeff Buckley) – A Little Like You (Grand Drive) – Live In A Hiding Place (Idlewild) – Lucky (Radiohead) – A Man Needs To Be Told (The Charlatans) – No Surprises (Radiohead) – Only Happy When It Rains (Garbage) – Out Of Time (Blur) – Painkiller (Turin Brakes) – Pass It On (The Coral) – Personal Jesus (Johnny Cash) – Pineapple Head (Crowded House) – Poor Misguided Fool (Starsailor) – Road Rage (Catatonia) – Seen The Light (Supergrass) – Seven Nation Army (The White Stripes) – Shine On (The House Of Love) – Silence Is Easy (Starsailor) – Sk8ter Boi (Avril Lavigne) – Stay Away From Me (The Star Spangles) – There There (Radiohead) – Thinking About Tomorrow (Beth Orton) – This Is How It Feels (Inspiral Carpets) – Wake Up Boo! (The Boo Radleys) – Words (Doves) – Yoshimi Battles The Pink Robots (Flaming Lips) – You're So Pretty – We're So Pretty (The Charlatans) – You've Got Her In Your Pocket (The White Stripes)

Essential Acoustic Playlist
9701A   VC   ISBN: 1-84328-207-0

All The Small Things (Blink 182) – All You Good Good People (Embrace) – Angie (The Rolling Stones) – Any Day Now (Elbow) – Bittersweet Symphony (The Verve) – Buddy (Lemonheads) – Burning Down The House (Talking Heads) – Central Reservation (Beth Orton) – Come Together (Primal Scream) – Cryin' (Aerosmith) – Don't Dream It's Over (Crowded House) – The Drugs Don't Work (The Verve) – Empty At The End (Electric Soft Parade) – Everybody Hurts (R.E.M.) – Everyday Is Like Sunday (Morrissey) – Fast Car (Tracey Chapman) – Fat Lip (Sum 41) – Fell In Love With A Girl (The White Stripes) – Fireworks (Embrace) – Fly Away (Lenny Kravitz) – Future Boy (Turin Brakes) – Going Places (Teenage Fanclub) – Good Riddance (Green Day) – Heaven Knows I'm Miserable Now (The Smiths) – Hotel California (The Eagles) – Hotel Yorba (The White Stripes) – Hunter (Dido) – It's A Shame About Ray (Lemonheads) – Karma Police (Radiohead) – Kiss Me (Sixpence None The Richer) – Losing My Religion (R.E.M.) – Love Burns (Black Rebel Motorcycle Club) – The Man Who Told Everything (Doves) – Mansize Rooster (Supergrass) – Mellow Doubt (Teenage Fanclub) – Movin' On Up (Primal Scream) – Mr. Jones (Counting Crows) – Next Year (Foo Fighters) – Novocaine For The Soul (Eels) – Over The Rainbow (Eva Cassidy) – Panic (The Smiths) – Porcelain (Moby) – Pounding (Doves) – Powder Blue (Elbow) – Rhythm & Blues Alibi (Gomez) – Save Tonight (Eagle Eye Cherry) – Silent Sigh (Badly Drawn Boy) – Secret Smile (Semisonic) – Shot Shot (Gomez) – Silent To The Dark (Electric Soft Parade) – Slight Return (The Bluetones) – Soak Up The Sun (Sheryl Crow) – Something In My Eye (Ed Harcourt) – Something To Talk About (Badly Drawn Boy) – Song 2 (Blur) – Song For The Lovers (Richard Ashcroft) – Standing Still (Jewel) – Street Spirit (Fade Out) (Radiohead) – Teenage Dirtbag (Wheatus) – Tender (Blur) – There Goes The Fear (Doves) – Time In A Bottle (Jim Croce) – Underdog (Save Me) (Turin Brakes) – Walking After You (Foo Fighters) – Warning (Green Day) – Waterloo Sunset (The Kinks) – Weather With You (Crowded House) – Wicked Game (Chris Isaak) – Wild Wood (Paul Weller)

Classic Acoustic Playlist
9806A   VC   ISBN: 1-84328-332-8

Ain't No Sunshine (Bill Withers) – All Tomorrow's Parties (The Velvet Underground) – Alone Again Or (Love) – Another Brick In The Wall Part II (Pink Floyd) – Bad Moon Rising (Creedence Clearwater Revival) – Black Magic Woman (Fleetwood Mac) – Both Sides Now (Joni Mitchell) – Brain Damage/Eclipse (Pink Floyd) – Break On Through (The Doors) – California Dreamin' (The Mamas & The Papas) – Cocaine (Eric Clapton) – Cosmic Dancer (T. Rex) – Crazy Little Thing Called Love (Queen) – Daydream Believer (The Monkees) – Days (The Kinks) – Desperado (The Eagles) – Eight Miles High (The Byrds) – Everybody's Talkin' (Harry Nilsson) – Five Years (David Bowie) – For What It's Worth (Buffalo Springfield) – Fortunate Son (Creedence Clearwater Revival) – Get It On (T. Rex) – Handbags & Gladrags (Rod Stewart) – Happy (The Rolling Stones) – He Ain't Heavy, He's My Brother (The Hollies) – Heroin (The Velvet Underground) – A Horse With No Name (America) – I Feel The Earth Move (Carole King) – It's Only Rock And Roll (The Rolling Stones) – It's Too Late (Carole King) – Itchycoo Park (The Small Faces) – Layla (Eric Clapton) – Leaving On A Jet Plane (John Denver) – Life On Mars (David Bowie) – Light My Fire (The Doors) – London Calling (The Clash) – Long Time Gone (Crosby, Stills & Nash) – Long Train Runnin' (The Doobie Brothers) – The Look Of Love (Dusty Springfield) – Lust For Life (Iggy Pop) – Maggie May (Rod Stewart) – Make Me Smile (Come Up And See Me) (Steve Harley & Cockney Rebel) – Miss You (The Rolling Stones) – Moondance (Van Morrison) – More Than A Feeling (Boston) – Mustang Sally (Wilson Pickett) – New Kid In Town (The Eagles) – Oliver's Army (Elvis Costello) – Pale Blue Eyes (The Velvet Underground) – Perfect Day (Lou Reed) – Silence Is Golden (The Tremeloes) – Sloop John B (The Beach Boys) – Smoke On The Water (Deep Purple) – Space Oddity (David Bowie) – Start Me Up (The Rolling Stones) – Strange Kind Of Woman (Deep Purple) – Stuck In The Middle With You (Stealers Wheel) – Summer In The City (Lovin' Spoonful) – Sunny Afternoon (The Kinks) – Suzanne (Leonard Cohen) – Sweet Home Alabama (Lynyrd Skynyrd) – Tempted (The Squeeze) – Tequila Sunrise (The Eagles) – Turn Turn Turn (The Byrds) – Venus In Furs (The Velvet Underground) – We Gotta Get Out Of This Place (The Animals) – Whiter Shade Of Pale (Procol Harum) – Wuthering Heights (Kate Bush) – You're My Best Friend (Queen) - You've Got A Friend (James Taylor)

Essential Acoustic Strumalong
9808A   BK/CD   ISBN: 1-84328-335-2

All You Good Good People (Embrace) - American English (Idlewild) – The Drugs Don't Work (The Verve) – Grace (Supergrass) – Handbags And Gladrags (Stereophonics) – Hotel Yorba (The White Stripes) – Karma Police (Radiohead) – Love Burns (Black Rebel Motorcycle Club) – Poor Misguided Fool (Starsailor) – Powder Blue (Elbow) – Silent Sigh (Badly Drawn Boy) – Silent To The Dark (The Electric Soft Parade) – Tender (Blur) – There Goes The Fear (Doves) – Underdog (Save Me) (Turin Brakes)

Classic Acoustic Strumalong
9844A   BK/CD   ISBN: 1-84328-397-2

Alone Again Or (Love) – Another Brick In The Wall Part II (Pink Floyd) – Cocaine (Eric Clapton) – Get It On (T. Rex) – Handbags And Gladrags (Rod Stewart) – London Calling (The Clash) – Lust For Life (Iggy Pop) – Make Me Smile (Come Up And See Me) (Steve Harley & Cockney Rebel) – Mustang Sally (Wilson Pickett) – Perfect Day (Lou Reed) – Start Me Up (The Rolling Stones) – Stuck In The Middle With You (Stealers Wheel) – Sunny Afternoon (The Kinks) – Venus In Furs (Velvet Underground) – Whiter Shade Of Pale (Procol Harum)

Available now in all good music shops

A203

Available Now
In all good music shops

MGARed 9699A ISBN1843282054

Papa Roach/Between Angels & Insects/Broken Home/Last ResortPuddle Of Mudd/Blurry/Control System Of A Down/Chop Suey Hoobastank/Crawling In The Dark Incubus/Drive/Pardon Me/Wish You Were Here Lost Prophets/The Fake Sound Of Progress Sum 41/Fat Lip/In Too Deep Creed/Higher Nickleback/How You Remind Me/Too Bad Linkin Park/In The End Staind/It's Been Awhile/Outside Slipknot/Left Behind/Wait & Bleed Jimmy Eat World/MiddleAlien Ant Farm/Movies/Smooth CriminalA/NothingBlink 182/The Rock ShowLimp Bizkit/Rollin'Disturbed/Shout 2000/VoicesMarilyn Manson/Tainted Love

MGABlue 9705A ISBN1843282089

Starsailor/Alcoholic/Good Souls/Poor Misguided FoolElbow/Asleep InThe Back/Newborn/Powder BlueThe Dandy Warhols/Bohemian Like You Feeder/Buck Rogers Vex Red/Can't SmileTurin Brakes/Emergency 72/Mind Over Money/Underdog (Save Me)The Electric Soft Parade/Empty At The End/Silent To The DarkThe White Stripes/Fell In Love With A Girl/Hotel YorbaRadiohead/Knives Out/Pyramid SongBlack Rebel Motorcycle Club/Love Burns/Spread Your LoveMercury Rev/Nite & FogHaven/Say SomethingHundred Reasons/Silver'The Coral/Skeleton KeyA/StarbucksThe Music/The People Doves/There Goes The FearMull Historical Society/Watching XanaduThe Cooper Temple Clause/ Who Needs Enemies Idlewild/You Held The World In Your Arms

MGABlack 9798A ISBN1843286661

Foo Fighters/All My LifeDrowning Pool/All Over MeDisturbed/Believe/Prayer/RememberAudioslave/ CochiseHoobastank/Crawling In The DarkRob Zombie/Demon SpeedingPuddle Of Mudd/Drift And Die/She Hates MeCrazy Town/Drowning Staind/FadeRaging Speedhorn/Fuck The Voodooman/The Hate SongFlaw/Get Up AgainOzzy Osbourne/Gets Me Through Ill Niño/God Save Us/UnrealSlipknot/My Plague/People = ShitDry Kill Logic/Nightmare MarilynManson/NobodiesKittie/Oracle/What I Always Wanted Slayer/ Perversions Of PainMudvayne/SeveredPapa Roach/She Loves Me Not/Time And Time AgainFilter/You Walk Away

MGAWhite 9856A ISBN1843284138

Badly Drawn Boy/All PossibilitiesJJ72/Always And ForeverMull Historical Society/Am I Wrong/The FinalArrearsTurin Brakes/Average Man/Long Distance/PainkillerRichard Ashcroft/Buy It In BottlesThe Mock Turtles/Can You Dig It British SeaPower/Carrion Blur/Crazy Beat/Out Of TimeThe Coral/Don't Think You're The First/Dreaming Of You The Flaming Lips/Fight Test/Yoshimi Battles The Pink RobotsStarsailor/Four To The Floor/Silence Is EasyLongview/Further'The White Stripes/I Want To Be The Boy To Warm Your Mother's Heart/You've Got Her In Your PocketThe Bees/A Minha MeninaIdlewild/A Modern Way Of Letting GoJohnny Cash/Personal JesusSupergrass/Rush Hour Soul/ Seen The LightThe Strokes/SomedayRooney/Stay AwayRadiohead/There There Beth Orton/Thinking About TomorrowThe Libertines/Up The Bracket

MGAPurple 9855A ISBN184328412X

Simple Plan/Addicted Good Charlotte/The Anthem/Girls And Boys/Lifestyles Of The Rich And FamousThe White Stripes/Ball And Biscuit/Seven Nation ArmyStone Sour/ Bother/InhaleEvanescence/Bring Me To LifeRadio 4/Eyes Wide OpenThe Kills/Fried My Little BrainsOK Go/Get Over ItA/Good Time Deftones/Hexagram/Minerva The Star Spangles/I Live For Speed/Stay Away From MeNickelback/Learn The Hard Way/ Someday Foo Fighters/LowKid Rock feat. Sheryl Crow/PictureStaind/Price To PlaySum41/ Still WaitingThe Donnas/Take It Off/Who Invited You?The Used/The Taste Of Ink Nirvana/You Know You're Right

Make Music With

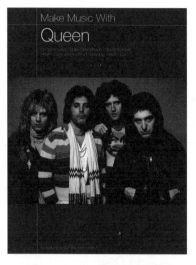
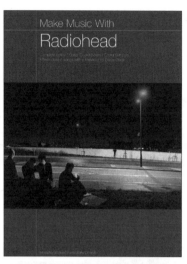
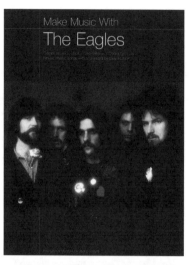

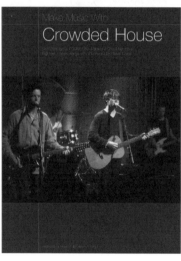

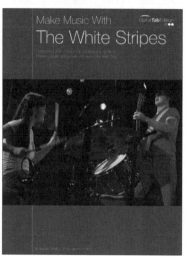

Queen
9698A MCL ISBN: 1-84328-204-6

Queen (Guitar Tablature Edition)
9836A GTAB ISBN: 1-84328-382-4

Radiohead
9708A MCL ISBN: 1-84328-211-9

Radiohead (Guitar Tablature Edition)
9835A GTAB ISBN: 1-84328-381-6

The Eagles
9802A MCL ISBN: 1-84328-325-5

Supergrass
9736A MCL ISBN: 1-84328-325-5

Crowded House
7291A MCL ISBN: 1-903692-37-7

The Verve
8862A MCL ISBN: 1-85909-875-4

The White Stripes
10028A MCL ISBN: 1-84328-716-1

**The White Stripes
(Guitar Tablature Edition)**
10029A GTAB ISBN: 1-84328-717-X

Available in all good music shops